B·L·E·S·S·I·N·G·S
FOR GOD'S PEOPLE

BLESSINGS
FOR GOD'S PEOPLE

A Book of Blessings
for All Occasions

REV. THOMAS G. SIMONS

AVE MARIA PRESS + Notre Dame, Indiana 46556

Permissions and credits:

Excerpts from *Come, Lord Jesus* by Lucien Deiss, C.S.Sp., copyright © 1981 by Lucien Deiss, C.S.Sp., reprinted with permission of World Library Publications.

Excerpts from "Home Blessings" and "Blessing for a New School Year," copyright © Worship Resources, Inc., 3015 Zuni St., Denver, CO 80211.

Psalm 134 from the *New American Bible*, copyright © 1970, by the Confraternity of Christian Doctrine, Washington D.C., is used by permission of copyright owner. All rights reserved.

"Canticle of Brother Sun," translated by Benan Fahy, O.F.M., in *Writings of St. Francis of Assisi*, copyright © 1964 by Franciscan Herald Press. Used with permission of the publisher.

"Epiphany House Blessing," copyright © 1981, Office of Liturgy, Diocese of Columbus. All rights reserved.

Excerpts from *Prayers for the Domestic Church* by Edward M. Hays, copyright © 1979 by Rev. Edward M. Hays, Forest of Peace Books, Easton, KS 66020.

Excerpts from the *Book of Occasional Services* used by permission of The Church Pension Fund.

"St. Blase Service" by James Wilbur, copyright by J.S. Paluch. Used with permission of the publisher.

Excerpts reprinted from *Lutheran Book of Worship*, copyright © 1978, Augsburg Publishing House.

Excerpts from *Liturgy 70*, Christmas 1977, Liturgy Training Publications, Archdiocese of Chicago.

Excerpts from the English translation of *Rite of Baptism for Children* © 1969, International Committee on English in the Liturgy, Inc. (ICEL); excerpts from the English translation of *The Roman Missal* © 1973, ICEL. All rights reserved.

© 1983 by Ave Maria Press, Notre Dame, Indiana 46556

All rights reserved. No part of this book may be used or reproduced in any manner whatsoever without written permission, except in the case of reprints in the context of reviews.

International Standard Book Number: 0-87793-264-6

Library of Congress Catalog Card Number: 82-62045

Cover design and art by Katherine Robinson

Printed and bound in the United States of America.

For the Basilica Parish of
Saint Adalbert in Grand Rapids
—a community of blessing for me.

About the Author:

Father Thomas Simons is Director of Worship for the Diocese of Grand Rapids, Michigan, where he has also served as an Associate Pastor in several parishes. His interest and expertise in the subject of blessings is reflected in his widely acclaimed book, *Blessings: A Reappraisal* (Resource Publications, 1981), and a number of articles in such publications as *Today's Parish, Homiletic and Pastoral Review, The Priest* and *Celebration.* His column, "Liturgy Things & Stuff," is a regular feature in *Modern Liturgy* magazine.

Contents

Introduction

I recently noticed a bread wrapper which proudly advertised, "Give your family the blessing of bran." I couldn't help but think that a lot of theology was being expressed in that promotional statement. We often use the word *blessing* (or *blessed*) to indicate good fortune or abundant favor. We also use it as a greeting or wish. In whatever way this word works its way into our vocabulary, it is rich in meaning and purpose.

Our Jewish ancestors knew of a deeply spiritual meaning and experience of blessing. The 18 benedictions, which probably find their origin as 18 suggestions, gradually became distinct blessing prayers. Hallowed by time and use, they remain a familiar part of Jewish piety and worship.

This tradition is based upon scripture which abounds with blessings. God is seen as the source of all goodness, the perfect blessing. Israel recognized this in creation, God's lasting blessing that enriches all life. God's involvement with the human person, and various persons in particular (Abraham, the prophets, kings), is marked with blessing. Blessing assumes a special place as a means of salvation in the covenant. God's people enjoyed blessing as long as they were faithful to the covenant. The scriptures admit of many variations upon the word *bless*, but basically, when the text speaks of the work of God, it means blessing; speaking of the works of persons, it means praise. The blessing of God is recognized when the human person responds with praise.

Jesus Christ is the epiphany of God's blessing in the fullness of human personhood. Jesus gives substance to God's blessing with the example of his own life. The healings, the feeding of people, the meals with his disciples—all have blessing at their foundation. Jesus identifies with the blessing tradition of his people and makes full use of it in his prayers of praise and thanksgiving.

The church, through the apostles, received this rich blessing heritage and practices it in the name of Jesus. The church calls down God's blessing upon people and upon whatever they do and whatever serves them. Blessings serve as signs; they direct our attention to God's active presence in and around us. Blessings are symbols by which we recognize God's creative power and goodness in nature and in the works of the human person. This recognition becomes the occasion to turn to God, thank him, praise him and call upon him for help. Blessings, therefore, imitate the sacraments. We are a people of signs, and the sacraments speak to us of decisive periods in our life when we encounter the Spirit of the living God in word and action. Blessings continue the meaning of the sacramental encounter in the course of daily living; they prolong, in a sense, the depth of the encounter and give expression to a life of faith. They offer us, at any time or moment, wherever we may be, the good news that the world and everything in it is mightily blessed by God.

The church in our time is once again recognizing the value of blessings and is anxious for them to be experienced in all areas of Christian living. With this in mind, the following suggestions are offered as ways of recapturing and renewing the best of our blessing tradition:

1. Blessings in the life of the parish or family strengthen and celebrate the common faith of all. Many of these blessings are related to or flow from the celebration of the sacraments. For example, in the Rite of Infant Baptism the minister traces the sign of the cross on the forehead of the child and invites the parents and godparents to do the same. Parents should continue to make use of this blessing upon their children. Likewise, parents could bless the engagement of their son or daughter by joining the families together for a blessing celebration.

2. There is a special significance to the blessings which are related to the seasons and celebrations of the church year. These seasonal blessings point out the central mysteries of faith more clearly; they bring about a closer union between believers and these mysteries. Quite simply, they bring the church into the home, school or parish, and vice versa. Such occasions might be marked by the blessing of the Advent wreath, the Christmas tree and creche, or Easter foods.

3. Since Christians know that without the Lord they can do nothing, they ask for the blessing of God for themselves and for others, especially in certain life situations—during illness, on birthdays, beginning school, an anniversary, a journey.

4. Daily living invites the blessing of God as a recognition of the splendor of his presence in the most ordinary moments. The blessing upon a new day, at a meal, before Sunday worship, and at night are just some of the everyday occasions to bless the Lord of blessing. Many of these blessings are prayed individually, with just a few words.

5. Things and places are blessed when, because of their particular nature or significance, they seem to be directed toward God, expressing our special thanks, or praise, or petition to God. They also represent our dependence upon God and our need for his protection. Such occasions may be celebrated by the blessing of the home or apartment, a vehicle, or objects of recreation.

6. Any initiated Christian may celebrate a blessing. When a minister of the church is involved, it may be appropriate for that person to lead the liturgy of blessing, especially if the occasion is of a more public nature. In the family situation, the parents or another family member serves as the leader.

While by no means exhaustive or exclusive, the blessing models offered in this small book touch upon many occasions in parish and family life which are open to prayer, blessing and celebration. I stress these as *models* because they serve as springboards for *your* adaptation and creativity. The blessings offered here draw upon a rich variety of sources and traditions. A basic structure, patterned upon the liturgy, is always offered:

1. A call to worship
2. Reading of God's Word
3. Intercessions or common prayer
4. Blessing prayer and gesture

The reading of the Word especially should form an integral part of any blessing liturgy. You are always free to choose scripture passages not included here. A blessing liturgy may be simple or solemn depending upon the occasion. It should enrich the way you are already praying.

When people compose their own blessing prayer, the main components should be: praise, thanksgiving, petition/intercession, blessing. These components may be arranged in a variety of ways depending on the occasion. In the blessing gesture, the spoken Word of God is made manifest. The sign of the cross, holy water, incense and the laying on of hands in blessing are some visible expressions of the Word.

The traditional meal blessing with which most Catholics are familiar begins, "Bless *us*, O Lord, and these thy gifts. . . ." Notice that we are first asking for a blessing upon ourselves. I hope this book will be a blessing for you and all who share it with you. St. Ambrose said it well:

You may not be rich, you may be unable to bequeath
any great possessions to your children, but one thing
you can give them—the heritage of your blessing.
And it is better to be blessed than to be rich.

May the richness of the Lord's blessing be upon you.

Rev. Thomas G. Simons

Daily Blessings

Blessing of the Morning Meal

All make the sign of the cross.

Leader: Blessed are you, O Lord, you have nourished me from my youth. You give food to all living things. Fill our hearts with joy and cheerfulness. Give us what we need, and enough left over so that we ourselves may do good in Jesus Christ our Lord, through whom be power, glory and honor to you for ever and ever.[1]

All: **Amen.**

———— or ————

Leader: Give us life, O Lord, through your gifts, and in your abundant goodness give us food through Christ our Lord.

All: **Amen.**

———— or ————

Leader: Bless, O Lord, your gifts which we are about to receive from your bounty. Through Christ our Lord.[2]

All: **Amen.**

———— or ————

Leader: O God, bless this morning meal and give to us the grace of your presence, that we may help those with whom we eat to experience the uniqueness of being loved and wanted by you, O Christ, and by those who express your love.

All: **Amen.**

———— or ————

Leader: Lord, as we gather to share our meal make us realize our oneness in you so that with the strength obtained from this meal we will be a source of strength for each other.

All: **Amen.**

Blessing of the Noon Meal

———The Angelus———

Leader: The angel of the Lord spoke to Mary.

All: **And she conceived by the Holy Spirit.
          Hail Mary. . .**

Leader: I am the servant of the Lord.

All: **Let it be done to me as you say.
          Hail Mary. . .**

Leader: The Word became flesh.

All: **And made his dwelling among us.
          Hail Mary. . .**

Leader: Pray for us, holy Mother of God.

All: **Make us worthy of the promises of Christ.**

Leader: Let us pray.

          Pour out your grace into our hearts, O Lord! By the voice of an
          angel we learned of the incarnation of Christ, your Son. Lead us,
          by his passion and his cross to the glory of the resurrection.
          Through the same Christ our Lord.

All: **Amen.**

Leader: Lord, bless us as we enjoy this midday nourishment. May it
          refresh us as we continue our efforts this day. And may it be to
          your glory and honor.

All: **Amen.**

Blessing of the Evening Meal

When all have gathered for supper, one of the family members lights a candle or candles in the center of the table.

Leader: The Lord be with you!

All: **And also with you!**

Leader: Let us give thanks to the Lord.

All: **For great is his magnificence and glory.**

Leader: We give you thanks, O God,
through your Son, Jesus Christ, our Lord,
for having enlightened us
by revealing to us the incorruptible light.
Having ended the course of this day
and reached the edge of night
having been filled by the light of day
which you create for our joy,
we now possess, through your kindness,
the evening light.
Therefore we praise you and glorify you
through your Son, Jesus Christ, our Lord.
Through him be glory, power and honor,
with the Holy Spirit, now and always
and for ever and ever.[3]

All: **Amen.**

The blessing of bread follows.

Leader: You are blessed, Lord our God,
king of the universe,
you who have brought bread forth
from the earth.[4]

Leader: O Lord Jesus Christ, Bread of Angels,
living bread unto eternal life,
bless this bread
as you blessed the five loaves in the
wilderness.

May all who eat it with reverence
attain through it good health
and the healing of body and spirit
which they so desire.[5]

All: **Amen.**

Other Seasonal Meal Blessings

ADVENT

Before the meal

Leader: May the Lord Jesus come!

All: **And this world pass away.**

Leader: Father in heaven, we thank you for these days of waiting and watching for the coming of your Son, Jesus the Christ. May our hearts be filled with love, peace and joy. We thank you and bless you for this food and drink, and all good things, through Christ our Lord.

All: **Amen.**

After the meal

Leader: Let us proclaim the Lord's coming.

All: **Eagerly we prepare to greet him with joy.**

Leader: Father God, you have revived our spirits and we are grateful. Be with the poor, the lonely, the suffering. May they be blessed with the advent of our God. Through Jesus our brother.

All: **Amen.**

CHRISTMAS

Before the meal

Leader: The Word was made flesh. Alleluia!

All: **And dwelled among us. Alleluia!**

Leader: Lord our God, we thank you for the gift of your Son who is the source of all our giving. We rejoice in the splendor and glory of his coming among us. We give thanks for this food and refreshment and for all good gifts that come from you, through Christ our Lord.

All: **Amen.**

After the meal

Leader: All the ends of the earth have seen the saving power of our God. Alleluia!

All: **The Lord has made known his salvation. Alleluia!**

Leader: Loving Father, you have shared the gift of your Son Jesus with us. May we share him with others, especially through our service and love for the poor, for he is the greatest gift we can give. This we ask through Jesus our Lord and brother.

All: **Amen.**

EPIPHANY

Before the meal

Leader: The kings of distant lands and from the isles bring gifts. Alleluia!

All: **They come bearing precious gifts. Alleluia!**

Leader: Heavenly Father, may you be enthroned upon our praises as we thank you for the King of kings, Jesus your Son. We bless you for so many gifts showered upon us, especially this food and drink before us. May we always be grateful to you, through Christ our Lord.

All: **Amen.**

After the meal

Leader: We see the Lord among us. Alleluia!

All: **He has gifted each of us with himself. Alleluia!**

Leader: Lord of all, you have made manifest your Son, Jesus Christ who is our Lord and Savior. Help us to manifest him to others, especially through our love to the unfortunate, the unwanted and the searching. This we ask through Jesus your Son.

All: **Amen.**

LENT

Before the meal

Leader: Christ was obedient unto death, even to death on the cross.

All: **By the cross he has redeemed the world.**

Leader: God of infinite love, look upon us your family for whom Jesus, your Son, willingly gave his life that all might live. Bless the food of our table and nourish us ever more on the love of your Son. You live and reign with your Son for ever and ever.

All: **Amen.**

After the meal

Leader: And I, if I am lifted up, will draw all people to myself.

All: **By the cross he has redeemed the world.**

Leader: We praise and thank you, Father, for the sacrifice of your Son, Jesus Christ. May his body, broken for us, and his blood, poured out for us, cause us to be Eucharist for others. Help us to share the victory of the cross with all who suffer and are persecuted. We make our prayer through Christ our Lord.

All: **Amen.**

HOLY WEEK

Before the meal

Leader: Jesus Christ is the light of the world.

All: **No darkness can extinguish him.**

Leader: Powerful God, your Son Jesus entered the darkness of death and rose victorious as the light of hope for the world. We bless you with uplifted hearts and hands and rejoice in the blessings around us, especially this good food. We come to you in Jesus, the Lamb slain for sinners.

All: **Amen.**

After the meal

Leader: Jesus Christ is victor!

All: **Christ has died, Christ is risen, Christ will come again.**

Leader: Blessed are you, God our Father, for you have blessed us with your Son, Jesus. He is the Lamb who has been slain for our sins and has won for us the freedom to be his brothers and sisters.

May our praise give you glory and cause us to share you and your Son with all who struggle for freedom. We ask this through Christ our Lord.

All: **Amen.**

EASTER

Before the meal

Leader: The Lord is risen, alleluia, alleluia.

All: **He is truly risen, alleluia, alleluia.**

Leader: Glorious Father, we rejoice that your Son and our brother, Jesus, is victorious over sin and death. Bless this good food that we share as we rejoice in his victory and give us the strength to share the good news of Easter with others. We ask this through Jesus Christ risen, now and forever.

All: **Amen.**

After the meal

Leader: Jesus Christ has been raised, alleluia, alleluia.

All: **We rejoice in his victory, alleluia, alleluia.**

Leader: Almighty God, we thank you for blessing us with your Son, Jesus. As we have rejoiced with him in this meal may our hearts long for the new and eternal banquet with Christ our risen brother. Help us to share the blessings of this table with others. Through Christ the risen Lord.

All: **Amen.**

ASCENSION

Before the meal

Leader: The Lord will return, alleluia!

All: **Just as he has said, alleluia!**

Leader: God our Father, we rejoice in the ascension of your Son who is our glory and our hope. May your blessing be upon us as we share this nourishment. Let this food fan our desire to share the heavenly banquet with Jesus the Christ in the eternal kingdom for ever and ever.

All: **Amen.**

After the meal

Leader: He is with us always, alleluia.

All: **To the end of time, alleluia.**

Leader: Father, in this meal we have a taste of the friendship that you have shown to us in your Son, Jesus. Help and strengthen us to follow Christ more closely and to uplift others in his life and love. We make this prayer in the name of Jesus.

All: **Amen.**

PENTECOST

Before the meal

Leader: Come, Creator Spirit.

All: **Fill us with your love.**

Leader: Father, we thank you for the gift of the Spirit poured out upon us. We ask you to bless us with the food we share. May it enliven our spirit. May we always hunger for the gifts and fruits of the Spirit and share your abundance with hearts full of love and gratitude. We make our prayer through Jesus and the Creator Spirit always and ever.

All: **Amen.**

After the meal

Leader: The Spirit of the Lord is upon us.

All: **His love is in our hearts.**

Leader: Father in heaven, you have blessed us with your living and loving Spirit. May the food we have shared invigorate us and cause us to share the blessings of the Spirit with everyone around us. Help us to radiate the warmth of the Spirit in all we do. We ask this through Jesus in the power of the Spirit, now and always.

All: **Amen.**

MARIAN FEAST

Before the meal

Leader: Hail Mary, full of grace.

All: **The Lord is with you.**

Leader: Lord God, we praise and thank you for Mary, the mother of your
          Son, Jesus. Bless our food and our conversation on this feast of
          (name the occasion). May we rejoice with Mary and her son, Jesus
          the Christ, now and always.

All: **Amen.**

After the meal

Leader: Blessed is the fruit of your womb.

All: **Blessed be Jesus forever.**

Leader: Father, we rejoice today with Mary who was chosen from among
          all women to be the mother of your Son. May we follow her ex-
          ample and take her advice to do whatever he tells us. Bless all our
          loved ones and the brothers and sisters we do not know. Through
          Christ our Lord.

All: **Amen. Hail Mary . . .**

PATRON SAINT DAY

Before the meal

Leader: You are praised in your saints.

All: **And glorified in their witness.**

Leader: Lord our God, today we honor *(name the family member, friend
          or guest)* who celebrates his(her) name day, the feast of *(name the
          saint or patron).* Bless this meal in which we keep festival with the
          holy ones who gave you praise through their life. May we give
          you praise now with Christ and his saints forevermore.

All: **Amen.**

After the meal

Leader: Blessed be the saints of God.

All: **Theirs is the crown of life.**

Leader: Father in heaven, we thank you for your presence on this day of St. *(name the saint or patron)*. May our celebration stir in us a desire to share in the friendship of the holy men, women and children who loved you in life and who are an example to us. We make our prayer in the name of Jesus.

All: **Amen.**

THANKSGIVING

Before the meal

Leader: The earth has yielded its fruit.

All: **God, our God, has blessed us.**

Leader: Father, God of goodness, you have given us this land and made it fruitful through the work of human hands. Bless this harvest of plenty. May it sustain our lives and draw us more closely to one another and to you in thanksgiving and praise. We make our prayer through Jesus Christ.

All: **Amen.**

After the meal

Leader: Give thanks always and everywhere.

All: **To the Father in the name of Jesus.**

Leader: Lord, we thank you for your many gifts and praise you as the source of all we have and are. Teach us to acknowledge always your blessings around us and to be thankful for the infinite expressions of your love. Help us to be generous with others as you are generous with us. We come to you in praise and thanksgiving through Jesus your Son.

All: **Amen.**

Morning Blessing

Rise and face the East, making the sign of the cross on the forehead, lips and breast. Pray:

> I thank you, everliving God, for
> reawakening my soul. Great is
> your mercy and your faithfulness.[6]

Then pray the *Canticle of Brother Sun*:

> Most high, all-powerful, all good, Lord!
>   All praise is yours, all glory, all honor
>   And all blessing.
>
> To you, alone, Most High, do they belong.
>   No mortal lips are worthy
>   To pronounce your name.
>
> All praise be yours, my Lord, through all that
>   you have made,
>   And first my lord Brother Sun,
>   Who brings the day; and light you give to us
>   through him.
>
> How beautiful is he, how radiant in all his splendor!
>   Of you, Most High, he bears the likeness.
>
> All praise be yours, my Lord, through Sister
>   Moon and Stars;
>   In the heavens you have made them, bright
>   And precious and fair.
>
> All praise be yours, my Lord, through Brothers
>   Wind and Air,
>   And fair and stormy, all the weather's moods,
>   By which you cherish all that you have made.
>
> All praise be yours, my Lord, through Sister Water,
>   So useful, lowly, precious and pure.
>
> All praise be yours, my Lord, through Brother Fire,
>   Through whom you brighten up the night.
>   How beautiful is he, how gay! Full of power
>   and strength.

All praise be yours, my Lord, through Sister
    Earth, our mother,
  Who feeds us in her sovereignty and produces
  Various fruits with colored flowers and herbs.

All praise be yours, my Lord, through those
    who grant pardon.
  For love of you; through those who endure
  Sickness and trial.

Happy those who endure in peace,
  By you, Most High, they will be crowned.

All praise be yours, my Lord, through Sister Death,
  From whose embrace no mortal can escape.

Woe to those who die in mortal sin!
  Happy those She finds doing your will!
  The second death can do no harm to them.

Praise and bless my Lord, and give him thanks,
  And serve him with great humility.[7]

—St. Francis of Assisi

Night Blessing

Before retiring, face the East and with hands raised, pray:

Come, bless the LORD,
   all you servants of the LORD
Who stand in the house of the LORD
   during the hours of night.
Lift up your hands toward the sanctuary
   and bless the LORD.
May the LORD bless you from Zion,
   the maker of heaven and earth.

—Psalm 134, NAB

———— or ————

Blessed are you, Lord, God of all creation
for you make the bonds of sleep to fall upon my eyes
and slumber on my eyelids.

May it be your will, O Lord my God and God of
my ancestors,
to allow me to lie down in peace
and to let me rise up again in peace

Let not my thoughts trouble me, nor fearful dreams,
but let my rest be perfect before you.[8]

———— or ————

Blessed be the Lord by day!
Blessed be the Lord by night!
Blessed be the Lord when we lie down!
Blessed be the Lord when we rise up!
For in your hands are all the souls of all the
   living and dead.
Into your hands, I commend my spirit.
You have redeemed me, O Lord God of truth.[9]

Then conclude with the **Divine Praises.**

Blessed be God.
Blessed be his holy name.
Blessed be Jesus Christ, true God and true man.
Blessed be the name of Jesus.
Blessed be his most sacred heart.
Blessed be his most precious blood.
Blessed be Jesus in the most holy sacrament of the altar.
Blessed be the Holy Spirit, the Consoler
Blessed be the great mother of God, Mary most holy
Blessed be her holy and immaculate conception
Blessed be her glorious assumption.
Blessed be the name of Mary, virgin and mother.
Blessed be St. Joseph, her most chaste spouse.
Blessed be God in his angels and in his saints.

Seal the night prayer by making the sign of the cross.

Weekly (Sunday) Blessings

Sunday Meal Blessing

When the family has gathered at the table, the mother or another in the family lights the candle and says:

Light and peace in the risen Jesus!

All pray silently for a few moments.

Leader: The Lord bless us and keep us.

All: **Amen.**

Leader: The Lord let his light shine upon us.

All: **Amen.**

Leader: The Lord grant us health and peace.

All: **Amen.**

Leader: We thank you, our Father,
for the life and knowledge
which you have revealed to us through
Jesus your Son.

All: **Glory be yours through all ages.**

Leader: Just as bread broken
was scattered on the hills,
then was gathered and became one,
so as we gather may we be made one,
for yours is glory and power through all ages.[10]

All: **Amen.**

The leader prays over the bread:

Blessed are you, Lord God of all creation.
Through your goodness we have this bread to eat,
which earth has given
and human hands have made.
Let it become for us a source of nourishment and strength.[11]

All: **Blessed be God forever.**

The bread is broken and shared by all.
The leader prays over a cup of wine:

> Blessed are you, Lord, God of all creation.
> Through your goodness we have this
> wine to drink, which earth has given
> and human hands have made.
> Let it become for us a source of refreshment and joy.[12]

All: **Blessed be God forever.**

The cup is passed and shared by all.

Blessing Before Reading Scripture

Make the sign of the cross on the forehead, lips and breast. Pray:

> Blessed Lord, who caused all the Holy Scriptures to be written
> for our learning: Grant that we may in such wise hear them,
> read, mark, learn and inwardly digest them, that by patience
> and comfort of the holy Word, we may embrace and ever hold
> fast the blessed hope of everlasting life, which you have given
> us in our Saviour Jesus Christ. Amen.[13]

*Read the scriptures, perhaps the readings to be proclaimed at Sunday
Eucharist. (If more than one person is present, the group could discuss the
readings.) A period of reflective silence would also be appropriate. Place the
book of the scriptures on a table between a candle and some burning incense,
if desired.*

Before taking leave the scriptures may be reverenced with a kiss.

Blessing Before Worship

Gather briefly for prayer before the Sunday Eucharist. Begin with a renewal of baptismal promises:

All: Lord Jesus Christ,
you are the king of the whole world.
All that was made was created for you.
Exercise your sovereign rights over me.
I renew my baptismal vows.
renouncing Satan with all his works and his false glamor,
and I promise to live as a good Christian.
In particular, I pledge myself to do all in my power
to make the rights of God and of your Church triumph in the
      world.
Divine Heart of Jesus,
I offer you whatever I do, however feeble,
to obtain that all human hearts may admit your sacred kingship,
so that the kingdom of your peace will be established
throughout the whole world.
Amen.[14]

—Pope Pius XI

Sprinkle everyone with holy water. Then one of the parents or another person prays:

> Almighty God, you pour out on all who desire it the spirit of grace and supplication. Deliver us, as we come into your presence, from cold hearts and wandering thoughts, that with steady minds and burning zeal we may worship you in spirit and in truth; through your Son, Jesus Christ our Lord.[15]

All: Amen.

————— or —————

O Lord, on this the lord of days, we ask you to open our minds and hearts to receive your Word and to make us thankful as we celebrate the memorial of your Son. As we blend with the larger body of your church, may we go forth in the joy and peace of your risen Son, Jesus.

All: **Amen.**

Parents may lay hands upon their children and bless each in their own words, or they may say:

Bless us, O God, with a reverent sense of your presence, that we may be at peace and may worship you with all our minds and spirit; through Jesus Christ our Lord.[16]

All: **Amen.**

Yearly Blessings

Blessing of Seeds (Springtime)

As springtime approaches, seeds may be blessed before planting.
The prayer leader greets all present and invites them to join in the blessing celebration.

CALL TO WORSHIP

Leader: Let us bless the Lord of all times and seasons.

All: **And give him thanks and praise.**

Leader: Let us listen to the Lord's Word.

One of those present reads one of the following scripture passages:

WORD SERVICE

Genesis 1:11-12   Genesis 2:4-9,15
Isaiah 55:10-11   Matthew 13:1-9
John 12:24-26   2 Corinthians 9:8-11
1 Corinthians 3:4-9

The prayer leader may offer some brief reflections on the proclaimed word.
Others may offer prayers of thanksgiving recognizing the goodness of God in creation. Then pray the blessing prayer.

BLESSING PRAYER

Leader: Praise to you, Lord our God, for you bring forth life from the earth. We ask you to bless these seeds that hold the promise of life. Send sunshine and showers to nurture their growth. Watch over these seeds so they grow to maturity. Help us to share the food, the fruit of these seeds, with all our sisters and brothers. We ask this in Jesus' name.

All: Amen.

——————— or ———————

Leader: Lord, we pray, bless these seeds and nurture them with good soil, strengthen them in the gentle movement of the wind, refresh them with rain from the heavens, and let them grow to full maturity for the good of body and soul. We ask this through Christ our Lord.[17]

All: **Amen.**

The seeds may be sprinkled with holy water. Then pray the Lord's Prayer together.

Blessing of the Harvest (Autumn)

As fruits and vegetables reach the conclusion of their natural season, pause to give thanks for the fruitfulness of the earth.

The prayer leader reminds those gathered of the occasion for the blessing celebration.

CALL TO WORSHIP

Leader: The Lord is bounteous with his blessings.

All: **To him belongs our thanksgiving.**

Leader: The Word of the Lord speaks to us.

WORD SERVICE

Read one or more of the following scriptures:

Genesis 8:20-22	Joel 2:21-24,26-27
Deuteronomy 8:7-18	Isaiah 55:8-12
Luke 12:15-21	

Discuss the passage or passages and their meaning for today, if desired.

Some of those gathered may offer thanksgiving prayers recognizing the handiwork of God in his creation. Then pray the blessing prayer.

BLESSING PRAYER

Leader: O Lord, Almighty God, you do not cease to give many riches in
            the rain that falls from heaven, and nourishment for life in the fer-
            tility of soil. We give thanks to you for the fruits of the land
            which we have harvested, and we pray that you bless and
            preserve these fruits which we have received from your hand.
            Help us to be mindful of the needs of others as we rejoice in the
            bounty of your goodness to us. We make this prayer through
            Christ our Lord.[18]

All: **Amen.**

———— or ————

Leader: O Lord, maker of all things, you open your hand and satisfy the desire of every living creature. We praise you for crowning the fields with your blessings and enabling us once more to gather in the fruits of the earth. Teach us to use your gifts carefully, that our land may continue to yield her increase; through your Son, Jesus Christ our Lord.[19]

All: **Amen.**

Blessing of the Advent Wreath

This celebration is for a simple Advent wreath blessing in the home (or, with slight adaptation, in the classroom).

Gather around the Advent wreath before the evening meal on Saturday and make the sign of the cross.

Parent: The Lord of Light has come to save us.

All: **Let us live in his light.**

Parent: Let us pray.

O God, our Father in heaven, by your Word all things are made holy. Send forth your blessing upon this Advent wreath, and grant that we who use it may prepare our hearts and minds well for the coming of your Son, Jesus. May we receive from you many blessings and graces for our family. We ask these things in the name of the same Christ, your Son, our Lord and Brother.

All: **Amen.**

Say the prayer of the week. Then light the candle.

FIRST WEEK

Parent: O Lord, stir up your might and come! Be our protector and liberator; rescue us from the dangers that threaten us because of our sins, and lead us to our salvation. You live and reign for ever and ever.

All: **Amen.**

One candle is lighted by the youngest child and left burning during the meal.

SECOND WEEK

Parent: O Lord, stir up our hearts to prepare the way of your only-begotten Son so that through his coming on earth we may serve you always with a pure intention. You live and reign for ever and ever.

All: **Amen.**

Two candles are lighted by the oldest child and left burning during the meal.

THIRD WEEK

Parent: Hear our prayers, O Lord, and enlighten the darkness of our minds by your coming on earth. You live and reign for ever and ever.

All: **Amen.**

Three candles are lighted by the mother or another child and left burning during the meal.

FOURTH WEEK

Parent: O Lord, stir up your might and come! Aid us with your powerful assistance so that through your grace and merciful forgiveness we may attain salvation, which now is hindered by our sins. You live and reign for ever and ever.

All: **Amen.**

All four candles are lighted by the father or another child and left burning during the meal.

CHRISTMAS DAY

Light all the candles, including a white candle placed in the center of the wreath.

Parent: Father,
        we are filled with new light
        by the coming of your Word among us.
        May the light of faith
        shine in our words and actions.
        Grant this through our Lord Jesus Christ, your Son, who lives and reigns with you and the Holy Spirit, one God, for ever and ever.[20]

All: **Amen.**

St. Nicholas' Day Blessing

St. Nicholas is the source for many of our present Christmas customs, especially that of gift giving. His feast is an appropriate time to express the spiritual aspects of giving and sharing and invites a celebration of blessing in his memory.

CALL TO WORSHIP

Leader: I will look after my sheep, says the Lord.

All: **And I will raise up a shepherd to pasture them.**

———— or ————

Leader: The Spirit of the Lord was upon him.

All: **To bring good news to the poor and to heal the brokenhearted.**

Leader: Let us pray.
All-powerful God,
you made St. Nicholas a bishop and leader of the Church
to inspire your people with his teaching and example.
May we give fitting honor to his memory
and always have the assistance of his prayers.
We ask this through our Lord Jesus Christ, your Son,
who lives and reigns with you and the Holy Spirit,
one God, for ever and ever.[21]

All: **Amen.**

WORD SERVICE

1 Peter 5:1-4
Hebrews 13:7-9a

The following summary of the life of St. Nicholas may be read and discussed.

St. Nicholas was born in Asia Minor. He was named bishop of Myra, a poor and rundown diocese. When his wealthy parents died, he gave his wealth to the poor and devoted himself to the conversion of sinners.

Once he heard that a man who had become very poor intended to abandon his three daughters to prostitution because he could not afford a dowry for them to be married. Nicholas, the story goes, on three occasions threw a bag of gold through the window into the room of the sleeping father. His daughters soon were married. Later the father came to Nicholas, fell at his feet and said, "Nicholas, you are my helper. You have delivered my soul and my daughters' souls from hell."

This story and his many other works of charity led to the tradition of giving presents on Nicholas' feast day and at Christmas in his name. The name Santa Claus, in fact, evolved from his name.

Nicholas died at Myra in 350. His popularity, already great, increased when his relics were brought to Bari, Italy, in 1087. Both the Eastern and Western churches honor him. St. Nicholas is the patron saint of Russia, Greece, Apulia, Sicily and Lorraine. He is regarded as the special patron of children. His feast is December 6.

INTERCESSIONS

Reader: For the gift of each person here.

All: **We give thanks.**

Reader: For the capacity to care and to share with those in need.

All: **We give thanks.**

Reader: For a holiday season of joy, hope and peace.

All: **We give thanks.**

BLESSING PRAYER

Leader: Gracious and good Lord, we bless you on this feast of St. Nicholas, your servant, who is an example to us of a life of charity and love. May we see in his life an invitation to imitate his good deeds. Make us always mindful of the needs of others and help us rejoice in the abundance of your goodness around us. Through Jesus our Lord.

All: **Amen.**

Share a special treat or exchange small gifts, if desired.

Blessing of the Christmas Tree and Creche

Blessing of the Christmas tree[22]

A Christmas tree affirms life in seasons of cold and gloom. By decorating it with objects that have been gathered over the years a family says something about its own special life. When decorated, the tree is a blessing to the home and deserves our blessing in return.

Decorate the tree, but ask each person to save one favorite ornament (or make a new one) to put on at the blessing. When the tree is complete, but before turning on its light, gather the family for a simple blessing. One person should prepare the brief scripture reading beforehand.

CALL TO WORSHIP

Leader: We come here to pray in the name of the Father and of the Son and of the Holy Spirit.

All: Amen.

WORD SERVICE

Psalm 96:11-12 or Ezekiel 17:22-24

Then, one by one, put an ornament on the tree saying:

May this Christmas tree bring the blessing of (mention the blessing desired for the family or the world).

BLESSING PRAYER

Leader: Let us pray.

Holy Lord, Father Almighty, Eternal God, you caused your Son, Our Lord Jesus Christ, to be planted like a tree of life in your church by being born of the Blessed Virgin Mary. We ask you to bless this tree that all who see it may be filled with a holy desire to be grafted as living branches onto the same Lord Jesus Christ, who lives and reigns with you, in the unity of the Holy Spirit, God, for ever and ever.

All: Amen.

——————— or ———————

Leader: All glory and praise to you, heavenly Father. We thank you for sending us your Son Jesus to be our brother. Bless us as we gather here, and bless our Christmas tree. Let its lights remind us of Jesus, who is the light of the world. Father, we love you, and we praise you through Christ our Lord.

All: **Amen.**

——————— or ———————

Leader: Father in heaven, we thank you for your goodness. Bless this tree that we have decorated in honor of your Son's birth among us. Let its lights remind us that he is Lord, and its decorations recall our joy. Grant that we may receive him as our savior, and continue to give you glory by our lives. We ask this, Father, in the name of Christ our Lord.

All: **Amen.**

——————— or ———————

Leader: Lord of the forest, maker of trees, we honor you as we dedicate this tree that it be a sign of Christmas. Green as life are its branches; soft as compassion are its needled leaves; strong as love is its trunk. May all trees be for us Christmas trees and trees of life. As sons and daughters of Adam and Eve, let us rejoice in this tree of life; may the spirit of kindness and love rest upon it.[23]

All: **Amen.**

Exchange a sign of peace. Then turn on the lights and sing a verse of "O Come, O Come, Emmanuel."

Blessing of the Creche[24]

On Christmas Eve gather the family together and set up the nativity scene except for the figure of the infant. Turn out the lights and sit quietly in darkness for some moments. Then, as one begins lighting the candles around the creche or around the room if the creche is under the Christmas tree, all hum or sing "O Come, O Come, Emmanuel." Emphasize the refrain, "Rejoice, rejoice. . . ." Tell the Christmas story or read it from Luke 2. Place the infant in the crib at the proper moment. Sing "Silent Night" or another favorite carol, then pray.

Leader: We praise you, Lord God of all creation, for you have brought us
            to this season of rejoicing, and have given us the story of the birth
            of Jesus. Through all the days of Christmas may these figures that
            tell that story be blessed, and may this place be filled with
            hospitality, joy, gentleness and thanksgiving to you. We ask this
            in the name of Jesus the Lord.

All: Amen.

——————— or ———————

Leader: Blessed are you, Lord God, king of all creation. We praise you for
            your love. We thank you because you have loved us so much that
            you sent your only Son to bring us eternal life. Bless this nativity
            scene that we have prepared, and let it be a reminder to us of the
            Lord Jesus, Son of God and Son of Mary. Father, we praise you
            through Christ our Lord.

All: Amen.

——————— or ———————

Leader: Heavenly Father, accept our thanks for all that you have done for
            us. May this scene of Christ's birth remind us of his love for you
            and for us. Fill our hearts with the faith of the shepherds and the
            peace of which the angels sang so that we may always understand
            Christmas as beginning and ending with Christ, our Redeemer.

All: Amen.

——————— or ———————

Leader: Lord, we pray before this Christmas crib, and await the feast of
            the birth of the Holy Child. Call forth the child from within each
            of us; cause us to wonder and to rejoice again in this most ancient
            feast. With the shepherds we come to the birth of Christ, seeking a
            simple celebration. The greatest gift will be ourselves given to you,
            Our God, and to each other. May the star of Bethlehem which
            shone brightly over the first crib stand guard over us filling us and
            all the earth with light and peace.[25]

All: Amen.

*The Christmas tree and creche can be sprinkled with holy water. Then join in
singing Christmas carols.*

Holy Family Day Blessing

On this feast pause to thank and bless the Lord for calling all families, like the holy family of Nazareth, to be one in God's love.

CALL TO WORSHIP

Leader: Come, let us bless the Lord.

All: **And praise his name.**

Leader: Let us pray.

God, our father and our mother, we thank you for the family of Mary, Joseph and Jesus. It was at home with his parents that Jesus grew in wisdom and age and your grace, that he learned to know the Law and the prophets and to do right and love goodness. Bless with strength and patience and good humor all who would make such homes today. We ask this in the name of Jesus the Lord.

WORD SERVICE

Read one of the following scripture passages:

Sirach 3:2-6
Colossians 3:12-21
Matthew 2:13-15,19-23
Luke 2:22-40 or 2:22,39-40
Luke 2:41-52

Follow the reading with a litany of petitions:

Leader: We now pray together that our many families may reflect the charity of the holy family and may be signs of God's saving presence in the world.

That we may always remember that our individual families are each a part of the family of man, and that we may have concern for one another.

All: **We pray to the Lord.**

Leader:	For our nation, the United States of America, which has given us so many advantages and so much of the goods of the world.
All:	**We pray to the Lord.**
Leader:	For families who are poor, who are hungry, who suffer from war or disease.
All:	**We pray to the Lord.**
Leader:	That all of us, members of Christian families, may follow our own proper path to holiness and sustain one another in grace throughout our lives.
All:	**We pray to the Lord.**
Leader:	For the members of our families who are not with us today, and for those whom God has called to himself.
All:	**We pray to the Lord.**

Other petitions may be added. Conclude with the Our Father, Hail Mary and Glory Be.

BLESSING PRAYER

Leader:	Father,
	help us to live as the holy family,
	united in respect and love.
	Bring us to the joy and peace of your eternal home.
	Grant this through our Lord Jesus Christ, your Son,
	who lives and reigns with you and the Holy Spirit,
	one God, for ever and ever.[26]
All:	**Amen.**

The members of the family then bless each other with a sign of the cross on the forehead and a hug.

New Year's Day Blessing

The beginning of a new year can be an appropriate time to ask God's blessings upon a new period of time in life.

Gather before the meal. All join in making the sign of the cross.

CALL TO WORSHIP

Leader: Let us bless the Lord of days.

All: **His are the times and the seasons.**

Leader: Let us pray.

O God our Creator, you have divided our life into days and seasons, and called us to acknowledge your providence year after year. Accept your people who come to offer their praises, and in your mercy, receive their prayers. Through Christ our Lord.[27]

All: **Amen.**

WORD SERVICE

Read one of the following scripture passages:

Ecclesiastes 3:1-15
Psalm 90
2 Corinthians 5:17; 6:2
Revelation 21:1-14,22-24

A brief litany of thanksgiving follows:

Leader: For the blessings, seen and unseen, of this past year.

All: **We thank you, Lord.**

Leader: For the gift of life and its fullness.

All: **We thank you, Lord.**

Leader: For the wisdom to number our days in the presence of our God.

All: **We thank you, Lord.**

Other thanksgiving prayers may be added. Conclude them with the Lord's Prayer.

BLESSING PRAYER

Leader: *(with hands extended over the family members)*:
Eternal Father, you have placed us in a world of space and time,
and through the events of our lives you bless us with your love.
Grant that in this new year we may know your presence, see your
love at work, and live in the light of the event which gives us joy
forever—the coming of your Son, Jesus Christ our Lord.[28]

All: **Amen.**

*The leader lays hands on each person and signs his or her forehead with the
cross. If desired, bless family and individual calendars with the following
prayer:*

Leader: Lord, you who live outside of time and reside in the imperishable
moment, we ask your blessing this New Year upon your gift to us
of time. Bless our calendars, these ordered lists of days, weeks and
months, of holidays, holy days, fasts and feasts. May they remind
us of birthdays and other gift-days as they teach us the secret that
all life is meant for celebration and contemplation. Bless, Lord,
this new year, each of its days and nights. Bless us with happy
seasons and long life. Grant to us, Lord, the New Year's gift of a
year of love.[29]

All: **Amen.**

Epiphany House Blessing[30]

Leader: Peace be in this place.

All: **And with all who enter here.**

THANKSGIVING OVER THE WATER

Leader: Blessed are you, Lord, God of all creation. You have blessed the
            earth with abundant water. May it be for us a pledge of cleansing
            and protection.

All: **Blessed be God forever.**

            *A member of the family takes the water and a sprig of greenery
            and sprinkles the rooms of the house and the people, while all say
            together:*

All: **I will pour out water upon the thirsty ground,
                and streams upon the dry land;
            I will pour out my spirit upon your offspring,
                and my blessing upon your descendants.**

THE INSCRIPTION

            19 + C M B + 8__(year)

*One person makes the inscription with chalk above the door, while another
proclaims the corresponding words.*

            The three wisemen,
C   Caspar,
M   Melchior, and
B   Balthasar
            followed the star of God's Son who became man
19   one thousand, nine hundred, and
8__   eighty-(year) years ago.
+   May Christ bless our dwelling
+   and remain with us throughout the new year.

ACCLAMATION

Leader: Lift up your heads, O gates!

All: **That the King of glory may come in.**

Leader: Who is the King of glory?

All: **The Lord of hosts. He is the King of glory!**

PRAYER

Leader: Almighty Father, incline your ear.
Bless us and all those who are gathered here.
Your angel send us,
Who will defend us,
And fill with Grace
All who dwell in this place.

All: **Amen.**

St. Blase's Day Blessing[31]

Read and discuss the story of St. Blase.

Blase, a physician who later became a bishop, died for the faith in 316. While in prison he healed a child who nearly died because of a fishbone in the throat. Due to this, and to other cures, people pray to him as a helper in sickness. The devotion spread from the Near East to Europe in the 800s; he became one of the most popular saints during the Middle Ages.

In central Europe and the Latin countries people receive a blessed bread stick on St. Blase's Day. They eat a bit of it whenever they have a sore throat. In Italy and Ireland it is customary to bless oil in honor of St. Blase. The priest touches people's throats with a dab of the oil, and they take some home for use when they are ill. The best-known custom, the blessing of throats, has been in use for centuries. The priest holds crossed candles under the chin or over the head of each person and says a prayer of blessing.

The legendary details of St. Blase's life and these customs grew out of faith in God and belief in the church's concern for human suffering. The blessing given this day is the church's gift to us. It asks God's care for our safety and health, and conveys the message of his fatherly love in our daily needs.

Perhaps the European custom of giving blessed bread (or oil, wine, water and fruit) can be adapted when blessing children. Some nuts, a small piece of fruit or hard candy given to the children after the blessing may remind them to thank God for the mouth and throat through which they breathe and speak, taste and swallow, and also serve as a reminder to care for the mouth and throat properly.

A song of praise may be sung by all.

GREETING

Leader: The favor of the Lord Jesus be with you.

All: **And also with you.**

WORD SERVICE

Reader: James 5:14-16   or   1 Kings 17:17-24
                                         Sirach 7:33-36
                                         2 Corinthians 4:10-18
                                         Matthew 8:14-17
                                         Matthew 9:1-8
                                         Luke 7:1-10
                                         Matthew 4:23-25
                                         John 5:1-8

HOMILY

It may be helpful to explain that the blessing is a sign of thanks for our throats, by which we breathe and speak, taste and swallow.

All come forward to receive the blessing from the parent or leader who lays hands on each person and says:

> *(Name)*, may God preserve you by the prayers of St. Blase from sore throats and all illness. Through Christ our Lord.

Response: Amen.

INTERCESSIONS

Remember others who are sick and in need of healing prayer.

Leader: For *(name or names)*, we pray to the Lord.

All: **Lord, hear our prayer.**

CLOSING PRAYER AND BLESSING

Leader: Ever living God, we celebrate the memory of St. Blase who died in witness to the gospel. Give us also the courage to be faithful in your service and the final joy of glory with you. We ask this through Christ our Lord.

All: **Amen.**

Leader: Every worthwhile gift comes from above.
              May God grant you health of mind and body,
              and strengthen you with every grace and blessing,
              that you may enjoy his favor in everlasting life.

All: **Amen.**

Leader: Blessed be the Lord.

All: **Now and forever.**

Lenten Meal Blessing

In addition to parish Lenten services, families and groups may wish to observe Lent at table with an atmosphere of prayer and renewal. Perhaps once or twice during Lent families and friends may join together for such a service.

Prepare the table with candles and simple Lenten foods in imitation of the Seder table at Passover time: salad, hard-boiled eggs, bread and drink.

CALL TO WORSHIP

To symbolize God's presence, the hostess lights the candles while saying:

> Blest be the Lord, the God of creation,
> who alone does wondrous deeds.

All: **Blest be his glorious name forever;**
may the whole earth be filled with his glory.

The host lifts his drink-filled cup and says:

> Blest be the Lord day by day.
> He bears our burdens; he is our salvation.

All: **Our help is from the Lord**
who made heaven and earth.

All drink from their cups.

WORD SERVICE

Reader: Deuteronomy 26:17-19
         Mark 12:28-34
         (or another reading)

The host passes around the salad, eggs, bread and drink. Conversation may be directed to topics of Lenten renewal or to everyday opportunities for Christian witness.

INTERCESSIONS

Reader: God our Father, you have gathered us around this table.
Let your Word shake us out of our easy ways
that we may repent and take positive steps in our witness to you.

That Lent may bring a return to the covenant
in which we love God and our neighbor as Jesus teaches,
we pray to the Lord.

All: **Lord, renew the face of the earth.**

Reader: That Lent may be a time for truth, justice and peace
in the decisions of state, national and world governments,
we pray to the Lord.

All: **Lord, renew the face of the earth.**

Reader: That Lent may be a time for positive efforts
toward renewal of our covenant promises to love,
we pray to the Lord.

All: **Lord, renew the face of the earth.**

Reader: That Lent may provide each family with time
to strengthen bonds of love and communication,
we pray to the Lord.

All: **Lord, renew the face of the earth.**

Reader: That Lent's prayers and sacrifices may bring relief
to those suffering from any need,
we pray to the Lord.

All: **Lord, renew the face of the earth.**

Other personal intentions may be added.

Leader: These are our prayers.
We join to them our promise to live Jesus' way of love.
We seal this prayer and promise with this last cup.

All drink. Then join in praying the Lord's Prayer.

When the meal is completed, the leader prays the blessing:[32]

Leader: The Father of mercies has given us an example of unselfish love
in the sufferings of his only Son.
Through your service of God and neighbor
may you receive his countless blessings.

All: **Amen.**

Leader:	You believe that by his dying Christ destroyed death for ever. May he give you everlasting life.
All:	**Amen.**
Leader:	He humbled himself for our sakes. May you follow his example and share in his resurrection.
All:	**Amen.**

Conclude by making the sign of the cross.

Blessing of a Family Easter Candle

Decorate a large candle and place it in the center of the table. Surround it with flowers. When all have gathered for Easter dinner, light the candle and make the sign of the cross.

CALL TO WORSHIP

Leader: Christ our Light!

All: **Thanks be to God.**

Leader: Blessed are you God, Father of all nations. You are the God of light, and in you there is no darkness. As we gather to rejoice in the risen life of your Son, Jesus, may our home, and those of our brothers and sisters, be bright with laughter and warm with love. We ask this in Jesus' name.

All: **Amen.**

WORD SERVICE

Read one of the following passages from scripture:

> Luke 24:1-6
> Matthew 28:1-7
> Mark 16:1-8
> John 20:19-23

INTERCESSIONS

Ask another family member to read the following prayers, pausing after each line for all to respond:

> **He is truly risen!**

Reader: Christ our Lord has been raised. . . .
Death no longer has hold over him. . . .
He lives a new life. . . .
Alleluia, alleluia. . . .
Praise to you, Lord of Life. . . .
Peace be to you. . . .

BLESSING OF THE CANDLE

Leader: May the light of Christ, rising in glory,
dispel the darkness of our hearts and minds.

Heavenly Father,
Accept this Easter candle,
a flame divided but undimmed,
a pillar of fire that glows to the honor of God.

Let it mingle with the lights of heaven
and continue bravely burning
to dispel the darkness of this night!

May the morning Star which never sets find this flame still burning:
Christ, that Morning Star, who came back from the dead,
and shed his peaceful light on all humanity,
your Son who lives and reigns for ever and ever.[33]

All: Amen.

Continue lighting the candle at meals during the 50-day period of rejoicing.
On Ascension, the leader prays:

Leader: God our Father,
make us joyful in the ascension of your Son Jesus Christ.
May we follow him into the new creation,
for his ascension is our glory and our hope.

We ask this through our Lord Jesus Christ, your Son.[34]

All: Amen.

On Pentecost, the leader prays:

Leader: Father in heaven,
fifty days have celebrated the fullness
of the mystery of your revealed love.

See your people gathered in prayer,
open to receive the Spirit's flame.
May it come to rest in our hearts
and disperse the divisions of word and tongue.
With one voice and one song
may we praise your name in joy and thanksgiving.

Grant this through Christ our Lord.[35]

All: Amen.

Blessing of Easter Foods

If the family is unable to go to the parish church where there is the blessing of Easter foods, the family may celebrate this blessing at home on Holy Saturday.

The Easter feast concluded the Lenten fast and the foods that were to be shared in the feast were blessed with joy and gratitude. The original foods blessed were those prescribed for the Passover meal of the Old Testament: lamb, bread, wine, bitter herbs. Other foods have since been added which "Christianize" the blessing.

CALL TO WORSHIP

All join in making the sign of the cross.

Leader: The Lord has freed us from our sins by his own blood.

All: **To him be glory and power for ever and ever.**

Leader: Let us pray.

Father, you give us food to share that we might be nourished and strengthened. Above all you have given us your Son, Jesus, who gave his life and continues to give his life as food for many. May our gratitude for this food give you praise, through Jesus, the bread of life.

All: **Amen.**

WORD SERVICE

One of the family members may read:

Exodus 12:1-8,11-14
Deuteronomy 8:7-19
Joel 2:21-24, 26-27
John 6:1-13

INTERCESSIONS

Reader: God is the giver of all good things, of every blessing. He lovingly provides us with what we need. That the Lord may bless us with daily bread, we pray.

All: **Father, we thank you.**

Reader: For those who hunger, that we may share with them what has been given to us, we pray.

All: **Father, we thank you.**

Reader: For all who work with the soil, that they may have a fruitful season, we pray.

All: **Father, we thank you.**

Reader: We mention now the needs in our own hearts . . . *(family members may add their personal intentions).*

Reader: Let us pray for our daily bread as Jesus taught us.

All pray the Our Father.

BLESSING PRAYER

Leader *(with hands extended over the food):*

O Lord, bless this food, created by you, that it may be a means of nourishment and festivity for us as we rejoice over the Easter victory of your Son. May each of us who partake of these foods be renewed in body and spirit, through Jesus our Paschal Lamb, who lives and rules for ever and ever.

All: **Amen.**

The food may be sprinkled with holy water. The leader may say a prayer of blessing over individual foods, following the traditional practice:

Blessing of the Paschal Lamb and Other Meats

Leader: Father of all goodness, we bless you for this lamb and these meat products. You commanded our ancestors in the faith to prepare a lamb on Passover night. May these meats prepared for our celebration in honor of the Passover of your Son from death to life remind us of the true Paschal Lamb by whose blood we are saved. May we enjoy these foods and obtain your blessing through the power of the cross and the resurrection of your Son. This we ask through him, our Risen Lord.

All: Amen.

Blessing of Bread

Leader: Father Almighty, may your blessing be upon this bread and all who partake of it. As with the many grains of wheat which have combined to form this loaf, may we be made one through the sharing of this food. We ask this through the risen Christ, the bread of life, the bread from heaven, who fulfills every hunger for ever and ever.

All: Amen.

Blessing of Eggs

Leader: Heavenly Father, let your blessing be upon these eggs. In them we see a sign of your Son rising to new life from the tomb. May we share them in thankful celebration of the resurrection of your Son Jesus, who lives with you for ever and ever.

All: Amen.

Blessing of Children's Easter Baskets

Leader: Loving Father, in joy we thank you for the Easter baskets which (*name the children*) ask your blessing upon. May they enjoy these Easter eggs and candy and all that these baskets contain as they celebrate the resurrection of Jesus, your Son and our Brother. May we always appreciate the gifts we receive and the joy you give us in sharing them through Christ our risen Lord.

All: Amen.

All may join in singing an Easter hymn.

Valentine's Day Blessing

In addition to sharing cards, gifts and other expressions of love on the feast day of St. Valentine, celebrate this day with a simple blessing.

CALL TO WORSHIP

Leader: God is love!

All: **And we who abide in love, abide in God.**

Leader: Father, bless the love that brings people together and grows ever stronger in our hearts. May all the messages that carry the name of your holy bishop Valentine be sent in good joy and received in delight. We ask this in the name of Jesus the Lord.[36]

All: **Amen.**

WORD SERVICE

Read one or more of the following:

> John 3:16
> John 15:9-14
> Romans 5:8
> Romans 8:35-39
> 1 Corinthians 13
> 1 John 3:1

The life of St. Valentine might be read from a biography of the saints, and then discussed.

INTERCESSIONS

Leader: For God's love which nurtures the heart.

All: **His love is everlasting.**

Leader: For the love of parents who helped us to love.

All: **His love is everlasting.**

Leader: For love which brings us peace and hope.

All: His love is everlasting.

Other intentions may be added by those present.

BLESSING PRAYER

Leader: May the peace of God which is beyond all understanding keep our hearts and minds in the knowledge and love of God and of his Son, our Lord Jesus Christ.

All: Amen.

Exchange an expression of peace.

Labor Day Blessing

Labor Day not only marks the conclusion of the summer, but also celebrates the goodness of work and the blessings of labor.

CALL TO WORSHIP

Leader: May the goodness of the Lord be upon us.

All: **And give success to the work of our hands (Ps 89:17).**

Leader: Let us pray.
God our Father,
by the labor of men and women you govern and guide to
    perfection
the work of creation.
Hear the prayers of your people
and give all people work that enhances their human dignity
and draws them closer to each other
in the service of their brothers and sisters.
We ask this in Jesus' name.[37]

All: **Amen.**

WORD SERVICE

Read one or more of the following scripture passages:

Genesis 2:4-9,15	John 4:34-38
2 Thessalonians 3:6-12,16	Amos 9:11-15
Genesis 1:1,2:4	Luke 5:1-11

INTERCESSIONS

Leader: For the labor of workers.

All: **We bless you, Lord.**

Leader: For the dignity of human work.

All: **We bless you, Lord.**

Leader: For the right to work.

All: We bless you, Lord.

Assemble and bless a variety of tools and work equipment.

BLESSING PRAYER

Leader: Almighty God, your son Jesus Christ dignified our labor by shar-
           ing our toil. Bless these instruments of labor and be with your
           people who use them. Make those who carry on the industries and
           commerce of this land responsive to your will; and to all of us,
           give pride in what we do and a just return for our labor. Through
           your Son, Jesus Christ our Lord.[38]

All: Amen.

All Saints' Day Blessing

On the feast of All Saints (or on a Saint's particular feast) we bless the Lord for the lives of those who witnessed him and ask that we might reflect their example. Highlights of the life of a particular saint being remembered may be shared before the blessing celebration or following the reading of the Word.

CALL TO WORSHIP

Leader: Let us rejoice in the Lord!

All: And bless him in his saints.

Leader: Let us pray.
           God our Father,
           source of all holiness,
           the work of your hands is manifest in your saints,
           the beauty of your truth is reflected in their faith.

           May we who aspire to have part in their joy
           be filled with the Spirit that blessed their lives,
           so that having shared their faith on earth
           we may also know their peace in your kingdom.

           Grant this through Christ our Lord.[39]

All: Amen.

WORD SERVICE

Read one of the following scripture passages:

> Matthew 5:1-12
> 1 John 3:1-3
> Revelation 7:2-4,9-14

INTERCESSIONS

Reader: Holy Mary, mother of God,

All: Pray for us.

Reader: St. John the Baptist,

All: **Pray for us.**

Reader: St. Joseph,

All: **Pray for us.**

Reader: Saint Peter and Saint Paul,

All: **Pray for us.**

Reader: *(Add the names of other saints, especially the patrons of the children, the church or the locality. Pause for the response after each name.)*

The litany concludes:

Reader: All you saints of God,

All: **Pray for us.**[40]

The leader may impose hands upon each person.

Leader: Almighty God, you have surrounded us with a great cloud of witnesses. Grant that we, encouraged by the good example of your saints(your servant, *name)* may persevere in running the race that is set before us, until at last we may attain to your eternal joy; through Jesus Christ, the pioneer and perfector of our faith, who lives and reigns with you and the Holy Spirit, one God, for ever and ever.[41]

All: **Amen.**

Share a special dessert or treat, if desired.

Blessing Upon Visiting a Grave

The church has traditionally remembered the deceased, especially during the month of November. The Feast of All Souls recalls the faithful departed and invites us to remember all who have fallen asleep in Christ.

CALL TO WORSHIP

Leader: Jesus died and rose again.

All: **The Father will bring with him those who have fallen asleep in Christ.**

——— or ———

Leader: Give them eternal rest, O Lord.

All: **And may your light shine on them forever.**

Leader: Let us pray.
Pause for silent prayer.
Merciful Father,
hear our prayers and console us.
As we renew our faith in your Son,
whom you raised from the dead,
strengthen our hope that all our departed brothers and sisters
will share in his resurrection,
who lives and reigns with you and the Holy Spirit,
one God, for ever and ever.[42]

All: **Amen.**

WORD SERVICE

Select one of the following:

Wisdom 3:1-9	Matthew 25:31-46
Isaiah 25:6,7-9	John 11:17-27
Romans 6:3-9	1 Corinthians 15:20-24,25-28

INTERCESSIONS

Reader: Jesus Christ is the firstborn from the dead.

All: **Glory to him!**

Reader: We believe we shall become like him.

All: **Glory to him!**

Reader: Our hope is in the Lord.

All: **Glory to him!**

All who have gathered may kneel at the graveside. The leader may bless those present, and the grave, with holy water as a reminder of our baptismal commitment to enter into the death and resurrection of Christ.

BLESSING PRAYER

Leader: Almighty God, we remember before you today your faithful servant *(name)*; and we pray that, having opened to him(her) the gates of larger life, you will receive him(her) more and more into your joyful service, that, with all who have faithfully served you in the past, he(she) may share in the eternal victory of Jesus Christ our Lord; who lives and reigns with you, in the unity of the Holy Spirit, one God, for ever and ever.[43]

All: **Amen.**

Place flowers at the grave, if desired, as a reminder of the life and love of the deceased person.

Occasional Blessings

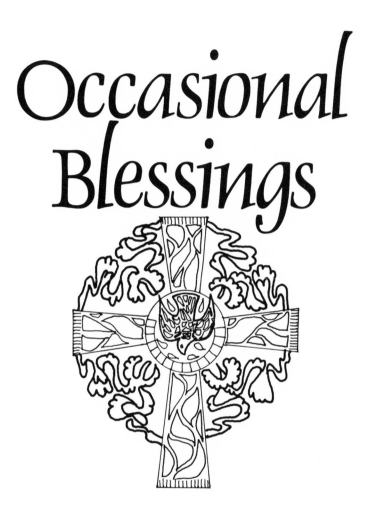

Blessing of the Home

This blessing may take place when a family moves into a new home or yearly as a re-dedication. Gather in the living room of the home.

CALL TO WORSHIP

Leader: Peace to this house.

All: **And to all who live here.**

Leader: Let us pray.
Almighty and everlasting God, grant to this home the grace of your presence, that you may be known to be the inhabitant of this dwelling, and the defender of this household. Through Jesus Christ our Lord, who with you and the Holy Spirit lives and reigns for ever and ever.[44]

All: **Amen.**

WORD SERVICE

One of the family members reads a passage from the family bible.

Genesis 18:1-8   Luke 10:38-42
Matthew 10:1,5-16   Romans 12:9-16

INTERCESSIONS

Reader: May the Lord bless us abundantly in his love.

All: **Blessed be God.**

Reader: May the Lord grant us the spirit of peace.

All: **Blessed be God.**

Reader: May we welcome all visitors here as Christ.

All: **Blessed be God.**

BLESSING PRAYER

The leader may sprinkle the house with holy water. An image of Christ or the holy family may be prominently placed.

Leader: Visit, O blessed Lord, this home with the gladness of your presence. Bless all who live here with the gift of your love; and grant that we may manifest your love (to each other and) to all whose lives we touch. May we grow in grace and in the knowledge and love of you; guide, comfort, and strengthen us, and preserve us in peace, O Jesus Christ, now and for ever.[45]

All: Amen.

——————— or ———————

Bless the rooms individually.

At the Entrance

Leader: Sovereign Lord, you are Alpha and Omega, the beginning and the end. Send your servants out from this place on many errands, be their constant companion on the way, and welcome them upon their return, so that coming and going they may be sustained by your presence. Through Christ our Lord.[46]

All: Amen.

In the Living Room or Family Room

Leader: Bless this living room that here we may find our bonds of friendship joyfully renewed and deepened after days of study and work, play and growth. May your peace always stay in this room, making it a place where we can each grow into better friends with you and with one another. Through Christ our Lord.[47]

All: Amen.

In the Kitchen

Leader: O Lord our God, you supply every need of ours according to your great riches. Bless the hands that work in this place, and give us grateful hearts for daily bread. Through Christ our Lord.[48]

All: Amen.

In the Dining Room or Area

Leader: Blessed are you, O Lord, King of the universe, for you give us food and drink to sustain our lives. Make us grateful for all your mercies, and mindful of the needs of others. Through Jesus Christ our Lord.[49]

All: Amen.

In a Bedroom

Leader: O God of life and love, the true rest of your people: Sanctify our hours of rest and refreshment, our sleeping and waking, and grant that strengthened by the indwelling of the Holy Spirit, we may rise to serve you all the days of our life. Through Jesus Christ our Lord.[50]

All: Amen.

In a Child's Room

Leader: Heavenly Father, your Son our Savior took children in his arms and blessed them. Embrace the child whose room this is with your unfailing love. Protect him(her) from all danger, and bring him(her) in safety to each new day, until he(she) greets with joy the great day of your kingdom. Through Jesus Christ our Lord.[51]

All: Amen.

In a Guest Room

Leader: Loving God, you have taught us to welcome one another as Christ welcomed us. Bless those who from time to time share the hospitality of this home. May your protective care shield them, the love of Jesus preserve them from all evil, and the guidance of your Holy Spirit keep them in the way that leads to eternal life. Through Jesus Christ our Lord.[52]

All: Amen.

In a Bathroom

Leader: Father, you gave us bodies that we might be the living body of Christ on earth. Grant a blessing which fills this room, so that out of love for you we may always care for our bodies as the living temples of your Holy Spirit. Through Christ our Lord.[53]

All: Amen.

Recreation Area or Backyard

Leader: Father, you richly shared your precious gift of life with us. Bless this place of rest and leisure time, that in our play and recreation, we may find refreshment and fulfillment for our busy lives. Through Christ our Lord.[54]

All: **Amen.**

In a Workroom or Workshop

Leader: O God, your blessed Son worked with his hands in the carpenter shop in Nazareth. Be present, we pray, with those who work in this place, that laboring as workers together with you, they may share the joy of your creation. Through Christ our Lord.[55]

All: **Amen.**

Exchange an embrace or a gesture of love. All may join in a song of praise.

Blessing of a Vehicle

Celebrate the following blessing upon the purchase of a new car or other vehicle (recreational or practical), or as a yearly blessing of vehicles in the parish. It may also be used prior to vacation travel.

CALL TO WORSHIP

Leader: The Lord be with you.

All: **And also with you.**

Leader: Let us pray.
Lord God, listen to our prayers as we ask your blessing upon this car(truck, boat, these vehicles). You have graciously provided for our needs in the past, so now we ask your blessing upon this vehicle(these vehicles) and our use of it(them). May all our travels and enjoyments lead us to you, our lasting joy. Through Christ our Lord.

All: **Amen.**

WORD SERVICE

Select from the following:

> Tobit 5:4-9
> Mark 6:30-32 or Mark 6:45-52 (blessing of a boat)
> John 14:5-7

INTERCESSIONS

Reader: Father, bless all who use this car(truck, boat, these vehicles). May they be conscious of their responsibility toward others.

All: **Lord, hear us.**

Reader: Help us to avoid all danger and accident by our carefulness.

All: **Lord, hear us.**

Reader: Protect us from harm and bring us back home in peace and joy.

All: **Lord, hear us.**

BLESSING PRAYER

Leader: Lord God, you are the maker of every good gift. You have seen fit to share with us the wonders of creation. We ask you now to bless this vehicle(these vehicles) and all who use it(them). May all who benefit by it(them) in their travels be responsible, always considerate and helpful to others. We make this prayer in Jesus' name.

All: **Amen.**

Bless the vehicle(s) with holy water, if desired. Families may want to place an image of Christ in their vehicle as a sign of dedication and a reminder of the Lord's presence and blessing.

Blessing Before Travel

Gather before a journey to invoke God's blessing upon the journey.

CALL TO WORSHIP

Leader: May the Lord be with us in our travels.

All: **And guide us in safety and joy.**

Leader: Let us pray.
Hear us, Lord, as we ask you to accompany us. May our journey help us to appreciate your creation and refresh us in body and spirit. May we reach our destination safely and return home in peace and joy. We ask this through Christ our Lord.

All: **Amen.**

WORD SERVICE

Select from the following:

> Genesis 28:10-15
> Tobit 5:4-7
> Luke 1:39-56
> Luke 3:1-6
> Luke 10:25-37

INTERCESSIONS

Reader: Let us ask God's blessing for each of us on our travels and for all who are travelling.
That you may safely guide us to our destination, we pray to the Lord.

All: **Lord, be with us.**

Reader: That your peace and protection may accompany us and all who travel today, we pray to the Lord.

All: **Lord, be with us.**

Reader: That we may always be considerate of others and mindful of safety, we pray to the Lord.

All: **Lord, be with us.**

Add other prayers, if desired. Conclude with the Lord's Prayer.

BLESSING PRAYER

The leader then prays over all:

Leader: May the Lord watch over us and guide us on our journey. May his saints and angels be with us to protect us on our way. May no harm come to us and may we reach our destination in peace and safety. And may we return safely with the Lord who is our companion and who is present to us always and everywhere.

All: **Amen.**

——— or ———

Leader: O God, we marvel at your providence which has given your holy angels care over us. You sent the archangel Raphael to accompany Tobiah on his journey. Grant that he may also watch over us in our travels. We believe that he stands before your throne. May he present our prayers for your blessing, that we may be safe under his protection and happy in his company for all eternity. We ask this through Christ our Lord.

All: **Amen.**

Leader: Let us go forth in peace and joy.

All: **Thanks be to God.**

Blessing Before Childbirth

Before the child is born, pray for a safe and happy delivery.

CALL TO WORSHIP

Leader: The Lord be with you.

All: **And also with you.**

Leader: Let us pray.
Loving Father, look with love upon *(name the mother)* and her child. Bless her husband, *(name)*, and guide them. May their child grow in wisdom, age and grace in your presence and before all people. We praise you, Father, and make this our prayer through Jesus your Son.

All: **Amen.**

WORD SERVICE

A family member or friend may choose one of the following:

Mark 9:35-37
Mark 10:13-16
Luke 1:39-45 (or 39-56)

INTERCESSIONS

Reader: Blessed are you, Lord God. You have blessed the union of *(name the parents)*.

All: **Amen.**

Reader: Blessed are you, Lord God. May this time of pregnancy be for *(name the parents)* months of drawing closer to you and to each other.

All: **Amen.**

Reader: Blessed are you, Lord God. May *(name the parents)* experience of birth be full of awe and wonder and the joy of sharing in your creation.[56]

All: **Amen.**

BLESSING PRAYER

Leader: O Lord and giver of life, receive our prayer for *(name the mother)*, and for the child she has conceived, that she and her husband, *(name)*, may happily come to the time of birth and, serving you in all things, may rejoice in your loving providence. We ask this through our Lord Jesus Christ, who lives and reigns with you and the Holy Spirit, one God, now and forever.

All: **Amen.**

Embrace the expectant parents. Gifts for the new child may be given.

Blessing of a Sick Person

Share this blessing with someone who is sick.

CALL TO WORSHIP

Leader: The Lord has truly borne our sufferings.

All: **He has carried all our sorrows.**

Leader: Let us pray.
O Lord our God, accept the fervent prayers of your people; in the multitude of your mercies look with compassion upon us and all who turn to you for help; for you are gracious, O lover of souls, and to you we give glory, Father, Son, and Holy Spirit, now and for ever.[57]

All: **Amen.**

WORD SERVICE

Read one of the following passages:

>Sirach 38:8-10,12-14
>Isaiah 53:1-5,10-11
>2 Corinthians 4:16-18
>James 5:14-16
>Luke 8:43-48
>Matthew 8:14-17
>Mark 5:21-24,35-42 (sick child)

INTERCESSIONS

Reader: God always answers prayers made in faith. We pray now for *(name)*, that the Lord may help him(her) in this illness.
God the Father, your will for all people is health and salvation.

All: **Lord, hear our prayer.**

Reader: Holy Trinity, one God, in you we live and move and have our being.

All: **Lord, hear our prayer.**

Reader: Lord, give *(name)* the security of knowing that he(she) is always in your care.

All: **Lord, hear our prayer.**

Other petitions may be added. Conclude with the Lord's Prayer.

BLESSING PRAYER

The leader may lay hands upon the sick person. Others, afterward, may do the same.

Leader: *(Name),* I lay my hands upon you in the name of the Father, and of the Son, and of the Holy Spirit, asking our Lord Jesus Christ to sustain you with his presence, to drive away all sickness of body and spirit, and to give you that victory of life and peace which will enable you to sense him both now and evermore.[58]

All: **Amen.**

For a Sick Child

Leader: Lord Jesus Christ, Good Shepherd of the sheep, you gather the lambs in your arms and carry them in your bosom: We commend to your loving care this child *(name)*. Relieve his(her) pain, guard him(her) from all danger, restore to him(her) your gifts of gladness and strength, and raise him(her) up to a life of service to you. Hear us, we pray, for your dear Name's sake.[59]

All: **Amen.**

Blessing of an Engagement

The decision to become engaged is a significant one in the life of a man and a woman, and offers an occasion for prayer. This blessing may be celebrated by the parents of the couple during a gathering of both families and close friends.

Begin, where appropriate, with the sign of the cross.

CALL TO WORSHIP

Leader: Let us bless the Lord for *(name the couple)*.

All: Praise to you, Lord Jesus Christ.

Leader: Let us pray.
            Father in heaven, your Son Jesus saw in the love man and woman have for each other the love he himself has for your church. May your love always be upon *(names)*, today, tomorrow and each day of their lives. We ask this through Christ our Lord.

All: Amen.

WORD SERVICE

Read one of the following passages:

>   Matthew 6:25-35
>   John 15:9-12
>   1 Corinthians 13:1-13
>   Philippians 2:1-4

INTERCESSIONS

Reader: Together let us bring before the Lord our needs and the needs of others.

Couple: We glorify you.

All: We praise you.

Reader:	That Jesus may be the foundation of love for *(names)* in their future together, we pray.
Couple:	We glorify you.
All:	**We praise you.**
Reader:	That divine providence may lead them to the bond of marriage, we pray.
Couple:	We glorify you.
All:	**We praise you.**

Add other intentions, if desired. Then join in praying the Lord's Prayer.

BLESSING PRAYER

The parents extend their hands over their children and pray as the leader says:

Leader:	Loving Father, we thank you for leading *(names)* to each other. As they desire to someday unite themselves to each other in marriage, may you now bless their intentions and keep them always close to you and your son Jesus, whose example of love is the source of all love, human and divine. We ask this through Christ our Lord.
All:	**Amen.**

If there is a ring to be exchanged, the man holds the ring as it is blessed.

Leader:	Almighty and eternal God, may this ring which symbolizes the hopes of *(names)* be a sign of their love for each other and for you. May God the Father, Son and Holy Spirit bless you always.
All:	**Amen.**
Leader:	Let us rejoice in the Lord.
All:	**His love is everlasting.**

Share expressions of peace and love.

Blessing on One's Birthday

A birthday is an occasion to bless God for the gift of life and love. Share in a blessing prayer during a birthday celebration.

CALL TO WORSHIP

Leader: It is with special joy and happiness that we all come together today to celebrate the birthday of *(name)*. May we all give our thanks to God for *(name)* life, and pray that he(she) will always know the greatness of his gifts of love.

Let us pray.

Father of every blessing, we bless you for the life that you have given *(name)*. May he(she) always know your love and continue to grow in age and wisdom. We join our love to yours for him(her) and make this prayer in Jesus' name.

All: **Amen.**

WORD SERVICE

The honored person or another may read the appropriate scripture passage.

Luke 2:6-16 (child's birthday)
Luke 2:41-52 (young person's birthday)
John 15:9-17 (adult's birthday)

INTERCESSIONS

Leader: We are glad that the gift of love is a part of the life of *(name)*. As the years go by may we all grow in our love and trust in each other.

All: **Hear us, Lord of life.**

Leader: For the many gifts and talents you have given to *(name)*. We have been enriched by them and blessed through him(her).

All: **Hear us, Lord of life.**

Leader: For all who celebrate the gift of life. May we always reverence the wonder of your creation in and around us.

All: **Hear us, Lord of life.**

All may join in praying the Lord's Prayer.

BLESSING PRAYER

Leader: O God, our times are in your hand. Look with favor, we pray, on your servant *(name)* as he(she) begins another year of life. Grant that he(she) may grow in wisdom and grace, and strengthen his(her) trust in your goodness all the days of his(her) life. Through Jesus Christ our Lord.[61]

All: **Amen.**

Embrace the birthday person. Share greetings and gifts.

Blessing Upon Retirement

This blessing is celebrated on the occasion of a retirement, to wish the person well as he or she begins a new chapter in life.

CALL TO WORSHIP

Leader: Glorify the Lord with me.

All: Let us praise his name.

Leader: Let us pray.
             Lord our God, we give you thanks for your gift of time. You bless each moment of our lives and fill it with meaning and purpose. Teach us to number our days so that we may harvest a rich life and know the rewards of our labors. We make this prayer through Christ our Lord.

All: Amen.

WORD SERVICE

The retiree or another family member or friend reads God's Word.

> Matthew 5:14-16
> Hebrews 6:10-12

> (or another scripture passage)

INTERCESSIONS

Reader: For every hour, minute and second, Father, that we may gain wisdom of heart.

All: You are praised.

Reader: For the opportunity to have served you in others and to reflect your goodness in work.

All: You are praised.

Reader: For *(name)*, that he(she) will find new meaning in life as he(she) continues to do your will.

All: **You are praised.**

Other prayers may be added. Then join in the Lord's Prayer.

BLESSING PRAYER

Leader: Lord God, you have blessed us with many gifts which we seek to put at the service of your kingdom. Bless *(name)*, as he(she) looks forward to a new and sturdy growth in life. Help him(her) to know retirement not as an end but as a beginning, to know the joy of a new and gentle work made in perfect love. Give him(her) health in mind, body and spirit so that the days to come will be a new creation, a new path. This we ask in the name of your Son, risen and living in each of us, guiding all our days.

All: **Amen.**

Embrace the retiree and offer good wishes. Gifts of gratitude may be given.

Blessing Upon Beginning a New Job

Share prayers and blessing, calling upon God for guidance and wisdom, upon beginning a new job.

CALL TO WORSHIP

Leader: I will bless the Lord at all times.

All: **His praise I will speak forever.**

Leader: Let us pray.
O God, ever generous and caring in all our needs, we thank you and bless you for guiding us on the journey of life and lighting the path of unknown ways. May our hearts trust the way you have prepared and help us to be generous in sharing your goodness. Through Christ our Lord.

All: **Amen.**

WORD SERVICE

   2 Corinthians 6:1-3
   Matthew 25:14-30

   (other scripture passages may be chosen as well)

INTERCESSIONS

Reader: Bless *(name)*, as he(she) begins a new job and give him(her) the grace and strength to carry it out.

All: **Lord, hear us.**

Reader: Bless us, help us to support one another in our efforts and endeavors.

All: **Lord, hear us.**

Reader: Bless all who begin new paths in daily work and living; guide them in your truth.

All: **Lord, hear us.**

BLESSING PRAYER

Leader: Lord of heaven and earth, we give you the glory due your holy name. We call on your name to bless *(name)*, as he(she) begins a new job(position/assignment). Give him(her) the needed guidance so that his(her) efforts will be fruitful and valuable. May all our efforts build up your kingdom where you live with Jesus and the Spirit, for ever and ever.

All: **Amen.**

Family and friends share in congratulating their relative or friend. A special dessert or a toast can be shared to commemorate the occasion.

Blessing on the Baptismal Anniversary

The baptismal anniversary is an occasion to renew baptismal vows and to bless God for the grace of redemption in Christ. The person's baptismal candle may be placed in the room, along with other mementos of the baptism. The blessing celebration may also take place within the context of a meal.

CALL TO WORSHIP

Leader: I have called you by name, says the Lord.

All: **You are mine forever.**

Leader: Let us pray.
            Gracious Lord, we bless you as we recall the day of *(name)* baptism. On this day you called him(her) to be your son(daughter) and to be one with Christ in your church. May each of us cherish the memory of our baptism as the day of new birth by water and the spirit. We make this prayer through Christ our Lord.

All: **Amen.**

Sprinkle everyone with holy water and make the sign of the cross.

WORD SERVICE

Choose from the following passages:

>   Ezekiel 36:24-28
>   Mark 1:9-11
>   John 7:37-39
>   Romans 6:3-5
>   1 Corinthians 12:12-13

INTERCESSIONS

Reader: Lead us by a holy life to the joys of God's kingdom, we pray.

All: **Lord, hear our prayer.**

Reader: Keep our family always in your love, we pray.

All: **Lord, hear our prayer.**

Reader: Renew the grace of our baptism in each one of us, we pray.

All: **Lord, hear our prayer.**[62]

Pray together the Apostles' Creed or the Nicene Creed.

BLESSING PRAYER

The leader lays his or her hands upon the person's head and prays:

Leader: *(Name),* we commend you to the mercy and grace of God our almighty Father, of his only Son, and of the Holy Spirit. May he protect your path, so that walking in the light of faith, you may come to the good things he has promised us. Through Christ our Lord.[63]

All: **Amen.**

Exchange a sign of love and peace. A song may be sung by all.

Blessing Upon the New School Year[64]

Gather some symbols of summer—a swimming certificate, a tennis ball, a jar of preserves, a map of a summer trip. Place these on a table with symbols of school—text books, lunch boxes, ruler, pencils.

CALL TO WORSHIP

Leader: Summer has been a time for new adventures, for relaxing recreation and for informal learning. As we share what we have gained from this summer, let us remember that God our Father has given us minds and hearts to grow so that we can become fuller persons and thus more like his Son, Jesus.

At this point, encourage some participants to share a symbol of the summer and describe what he or she learned about self and life from the activity connected with the symbol.

Leader: Thanksgiving is the most important attitude we can have toward God. We call Jesus' gift of himself to us *Eucharist*, which means thanksgiving or, perhaps better, thanks-living. Let us remember the happenings of our summer and thank our Father for them, as we respond: Thank you, Father!

For friends we visited or who visited us, sharing their life with us, we say . . .

For vacations and gardens, for ball games and bike riding, for swimming and suntans, we say . . .

For the sun and wind and rain, for lakes and mountains and prairies, for grass and flowers and trees and blue skies, we say . . .

Add other "Thank you's," if desired.

Leader: Father, we bring before you the joys of summer. We remember that all life comes from you and that we share your life in learning and loving your creation. Thank you for the gift of life in your Son. May the coming months bring us closer to you, through Jesus, our brother and Lord.

All: Amen.

WORD SERVICE

Leader: The informal learning we shared this summer becomes more formal when school begins. Each year brings the opportunity to grow and to become richer in knowledge through new classes, teachers, books and experiences. Each new school year permits us to make important choices about how we use or abuse time in class and in life. We can decide how to use the next nine months for growth or for wasting. Listen to a reading which prompts us to seek wisdom.

Reader: Proverbs 8:32-36

Discussion may follow, depending on the age of the children.

Leader: Let us spend a few moments in silent reflection. What do we hope to gain from the coming school year? Let us also prepare to share our prayer for the coming school year.

Allow time for silent reflection and preparation for prayer.

INTERCESSIONS

Leader: We bring our hopes and fears about school before you, Father, knowing that you want only our growth as persons beloved by your Son, Jesus.

Participants may share their prayers for the year.

Leader: Father, we know that your strength will be with us in the coming months. We want to make them months of growth and learning, but we sometimes get lazy and do not make the necessary effort. When this happens, remind us that with your love we can do all things. With your grace, tasks and assignments which seem to be almost impossible become possible and joyful. We know you will be with us, through your Son, Jesus.

All: **Amen.**

BLESSING PRAYER

Leader: May the Lord walk behind you and before you. May his strength be a light to you this year, and may he bless you through Jesus!

Person: **Amen!**

Blessing on an Anniversary (Marriage, Ordination, Vows)

This blessing may be celebrated in conjunction with a dinner celebration or gathering.

CALL TO WORSHIP

Leader: Proclaim with me the greatness of the Lord.

All: Together let us bless his name.

Leader: Let us pray.   Let us pray.

            (for married couple)   (for clergy/religious)

God our Father,
you created man and woman
to love each other
in the bond of marriage.
Bless and strengthen *(names)*.
May their marriage become an
increasingly more perfect sign
of the union between Christ
and his Church.

We ask this through our Lord
Jesus Christ.[65]

All: Amen.

O Lord Jesus Christ, you
became poor for our sake, that
we might be made rich through
your poverty. Guide and sanctify, we pray, those whom you
call to follow you under the
vows (promises) of poverty,
celibacy, and obedience, that
by their prayer and service they
may enrich your Church, and
by their life and worship may
glorify your Name. You reign
with the Father and the Holy
Spirit, one God, now and
forever.[66]

All: Amen.

WORD SERVICE

Select from the following passages:

(Marriage)
Genesis 1:26-28,31
1 Corinthians 12:31-13:8
Ephesians 5:25-33
Colossians 3:12-17
Mark 10:6-9
John 2:1-11

(Orders/Vows)
Isaiah 61:1-3
Acts 10:37-43
Romans 12:4-8
Matthew 20:25-28
Mark 10:17-31

INTERCESSIONS

Leader: For the covenant of love that you have established between us.

All: **We thank you, Lord.**

Leader: For the love of family and friends.

All: **We thank you, Lord.**

Leader: For the grace to continue serving the Lord with steadfast love.

All: **We thank you, Lord.**

RENEWAL OF COMMITMENT

The following renewal of promises is made separately by husband and wife:

(Name of husband or wife), (number of years) years ago I circled your finger with this ring as a sign of unbroken love and as a promise of care and concern without end.

Today, I repeat that promise and take you again to myself as God's gift.

Place ring on spouse's finger.

We are one body and one life in Christ, come what may, now and forever.[67]

All: **Amen.**

The following renewal of promises is made by the clergy or religious, adapting where necessary:

My brothers and sisters, *(number of years)* years ago, I freely and fully gave myself to the service of Christ and of his body, the church.

Today, with gladness, I repeat the promise(vow) of poverty, celibacy and obedience for the sake of the kingdom.

May God who began this good work in me bring it to completion.

All: **Amen.**

BLESSING PRAYER

(for married couple)

(for clergy/religious)

All present may extend their hands over the couple.

Leader:

Father, you have blessed and sustained *(names)* in the bond of marriage. Continue to increase their love in the joys and sorrows of life, and help them grow in holiness all their days. We ask this through Christ our Lord.

All: **Amen.**

God our Father, guide of humanity and ruler of creation, look upon your servant *(name)* who wishes to renew his(her) offering of self to you. As the years pass by, help him(her) to enter more deeply into the mystery of the church and to dedicate himself(herself) more generously to the good of humanity. We ask this through Christ our Lord.

All: **Amen.**

Pray together the Lord's Prayer. Embrace the person or persons celebrating the anniversary.

Blessing of Pets

This blessing may take place after Mass or at a separate celebration, perhaps on the feast of St. Francis of Assisi.

Join in an opening song.

CALL TO WORSHIP

Leader: Bless the Lord, all you his creatures.

All: **And forget not all his benefits.**

Leader: Let us pray.
O God, you have made us and these pets and all living things. You are even more wonderful than the things you have made. We thank you for giving us these pets who give us joy. As you take care of us, so also we ask that we might take care of our pets who trust us to take care of them. By doing this, we share in your own love for all creation. We ask this in Jesus' name.

All: **Amen.**

WORD SERVICE

Select from the following scripture passages:

> Genesis 1:24-31
> Psalm 104:10-25
> Matthew 6:26

INTERCESSIONS

Leader: For all your creatures that breathe and move and have life.

All: **Thank you, Lord.**

Leader: That we may love and honor the works of God's hand.

All: **Thank you, Lord.**

Leader: That each pet here may be treasured with care.

All: **Thank you, Lord.**

BLESSING PRAYER

Leader: Most high, almighty Lord, our Father,
Yours are the praise, the glory, the honor and
    all blessings!
To you alone, Father, do all things belong.
Be praised, Father, for giving us the animals,
    birds, and fish which fill your world.
Father, may we think of you and thank you
    when we play with or care for our pets.
Be praised, Father, for making us so happy to
    have our pets and to have them to play with.
We ask you, Father, that we may be good to our
    pets always, so that they may be happy also.
Help us always to take care of our pets so that they
    will be healthy.
Father, your world is wonderful. May we all
    come into your even greater world of the
    kingdom of heaven where we shall see even
    greater things and where we shall all live and
    love forever.
We ask this through Christ our Lord.[68]

All: **Amen.**

A concluding song may be sung and the animals sprinkled with holy water.

Brief Scriptural Blessings

Brief Scriptural Blessings[69]

Blessed be you, Lord, God of tenderness and
    compassion, rich in kindness and faithfulness,
who keep us in your love forever! *(Ex 34:67)*.

The Lord our God is a God of mercy.
To him be glory forever! *(Dt 4:31)*.

May the Lord bless us and keep us!
May the Lord let his face shine on us
    and be gracious to us!
May the Lord show his face to us
    and give us his peace! *(Nm 6:24-26)*.

Blessed be our God from everlasting to everlasting!
    And blessed be your name of glory,
which surpasses all blessing and praise! *(Neh 9:5)*.

Blessed be God!
Blessed be his great name!
Blessed be all his holy angels!
Blessed be his great name forevermore!
Blessed be all his angels forever! *(Tb 11:14)*.

Blessed be the Lord, the God of Israel,
    who alone performs marvels!
Blessed forever be his glorious name!
May the whole world be filled with his glory! *(Ps 72:18-19)*.

Blessed be you, Lord,
God of the humble and help of the oppressed!
   Blessed be you, Lord,
support of the weak and refuge of the forsaken!
   Blessed be you, Lord,
savior of the despairing—to you be eternal glory! *(Jdt 9:11)*.

Blessed be you, Father, Lord of heaven and earth!
You hide your mystery from the learned and clever,
but you reveal it to mere children.
Yes, Father, for such is your gracious will *(Mt 11:25-26)*.

May you be blessed, Lord Jesus,
who died for our sins
and rose again for our life!
To you be glory forever! *(Rom 4:25)*.

Blessed be the God of hope and consolation!
May he help us all to be tolerant with one another,
following the example of Jesus Christ!
So that, united in mind and voice, we may give glory
to the God and Father of our Lord Jesus Christ! *(Rom 15:5-6)*.

May the God of hope fill us
with every joy and with peace, in the faith!
May hope overflow in us
   through the power of the Holy Spirit *(Rom 16:25,27)*.

To the Father, who can give us the strength to live
according to the Gospel and the message of Jesus Christ,
to him, the God who alone is wise, through Jesus Christ,
be glory and power forever!
May God our Father strengthen us until the last day
   so that we may be without blame
   on the Day of our Lord Jesus Christ!
He is faithful, he who calls us
to fellowship with his Son Jesus, our Lord.
   To him be glory forever! *(1 Cor 1:8-9)*.

Let us give thanks to God, who gives us victory
   through our Lord Jesus Christ! *(1 Cor 15:57).*

Marana tha! Come, Lord Jesus!
Your grace be with us all! *(1 Cor 16:23-24).*

Blessed be the God and Father
of our Lord Jesus Christ,
a gentle Father and the God of all consolation
who comforts us in all our sorrows! *(2 Cor 1:3-4).*

Blessed be God our Father,
who raised his Son Jesus Christ to life!
He will raise us one day with him
and place us together by his side *(2 Cor 4:14).*

The grace of our Lord Jesus Christ,
the love of God the Father,
and the fellowship of the Holy Spirit
   be with us all! *(2 Cor 13:13).*

The grace and peace of God our Father
   and the Lord Jesus Christ!
He sacrificed himself for our sins
to rescue us from this present wicked world
   in accordance with the will of his Father.
To him be glory forever! *(Gal 1:3-5).*

Blessed be the God and Father
   of our Lord Jesus Christ,
who has filled us with blessings in Christ! *(Eph 1:3-4).*

Glory to God our Father,
from generation to generation,
in the Church and in Christ Jesus! *(Eph 3:21).*

May God the Father and the Lord Jesus
grant peace, love, and faith to all our brothers and sisters!
May grace be with all who love
   our Lord Jesus Christ! *(Eph 6:23-24).*

May God our Father,
who has begun an excellent work in us,
    see that it is finished
when the Day of Christ Jesus comes!
To him be glory forever! *(Phil 1:6).*

May the peace of God that is beyond all understanding
guard our hearts and our thoughts in Christ Jesus! *(Phil 4:7).*

May God our Father fulfill all our needs
according to his generosity, with magnificence,
    in Christ Jesus!
To him be glory forever! *(Phil 4:19-20).*

We give you thanks, our Father!
You call us to share the lot of the saints
    in light! *(Col 1:12).*

You rescue us from the power of darkness
and bring us into the Kingdom
    of your beloved Son *(Col 1:13).*

May the peace of God reign in our hearts,
that peace to which we are called together
    as parts of one Body.
In all our words and actions
let us give thanks to God our Father,
    in the name of the Lord Jesus *(Col 3:15-17).*

May God our Father put our faith into action,
to work for love, to preserve hope,
    through our Lord Jesus Christ *(1 Thes 1:2).*

May the Lord help us to grow and abound
    in love for one another.
May he confirm our hearts in holiness without blame
    before God our Father,
at the time of his coming with all his saints *(1 Thes 3:12-13).*

Blessed be God our Father,
who gives salvation through our Lord Jesus Christ.
He died and rose again for us
so that, awake or asleep,
we might live together with him *(1 Thes 5:9-10).*

May the Lord of peace himself
give us peace all the time
and in every way!
The Lord be with us all! *(2 Thes 3:16).*

Grace, mercy, and peace from God our Father
and Christ Jesus, our Lord! *(1 Tm 1:2).*

To the eternal King,
the immortal, invisible, and only God,
be honor and glory forever and ever! *(1 Tm 1:17).*

To the blessed and only ruler of all,
to the King of kings and Lord of lords,
who alone is immortal,
whose home is unapproachable light,
whom no man has ever seen or can see,
to him be honor and everlasting power! *(1 Tm 6:15-16).*

Jesus Christ, the same
yesterday, today, and forever.
To him be glory forever! *(Heb 13:8).*

May God be glorified in all things through Jesus Christ!
To him be glory and power forever and ever! *(1 Pt 4:11).*

May the God of all grace who has called us
to his everlasting glory in Christ Jesus,
after brief suffering,
restore us to himself and confirm us.
May he strengthen us and make us steadfast.
To him be power forever and ever! *(1 Pt 5:10-11).*

May grace and peace be given us in abundance
   as we come to know God
   and Jesus, our Lord!
To him be glory forever and ever! *(2 Pt 1:2).*

May we grow in the grace and knowledge
of our Lord and Savior, Jesus Christ!
To him be glory now and in eternity! *(2 Pt 3:18).*

To him who can keep you from falling
and bring you safely into his glorious presence,
innocent and happy,
to the only God, our Savior, through Jesus our Lord,
be glory, majesty, authority, and power,
from even before the beginning of time,
through the present,
and for all ages to come *(Jude 24-25).*

Praise, glory, and wisdom,
thanksgiving, honor, power, and strength,
   to our God
   forever and ever! *(Rv 7:12).*

Amen! Come, Lord Jesus!
May your grace be with us all! *(Rv 22:21).*

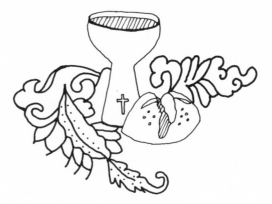

Footnotes

1. St. John Chrysostom, eighth century.
2. *Gelasian Sacramentary*, eighth century.
3. *The Lucernary*, Apostolic Tradition of Hippolytus, third century.
4. *Kiddush*, Jewish Sabbath Blessing.
5. Old Russian Prayer, *Family Festivals*, Resource Publications.
6. Jewish *Tephillah.*
7. St. Francis of Assisi, translated by Benen Fahy, O.F.M., in *Writings of St. Francis of Assisi*, Franciscan Herald Press.
8. Jewish Night Prayer.
9. Jewish Night Prayer.
10. Based on the prayer from the *Didache*, second century.
11. Adapted, *Sacramentary*, prayer for the preparation of the gifts.
12. Adapted, *Sacramentary*, prayer for the preparation of the gifts.
13. *Book of Common Prayer*, Episcopal Church.
14. *Praise Him!*, Ave Maria Press, p. 119.
15. *Lutheran Book of Worship.*
16. *Lutheran Book of Worship.*
17. Adapted, *Roman Ritual, Vol. III, The Blessings*, copyright © 1946, Bruce Publishing Co.
18. Adapted, *Roman Ritual, Vol. III, The Blessings*, copyright © 1946, Bruce Publishing Co.
19. *Lutheran Book of Worship.*
20. *Sacramentary*, Christmas Mass at Dawn.
21. *Sacramentary*, Common of Pastors.
22. From *Liturgy 70*, Christmas 1977, with adaptations and additions.
23. Adapted from *Prayers for the Domestic Church*, copyright © 1979 by Rev. Edward M. Hays, Forest of Peace Books, Easton KS 66020.
24. From *Liturgy 70*, Christmas 1977, with adaptations and additions.
25. Adapted from *Prayers for the Domestic Church*, copyright © 1979 by Rev. Edward M. Hays, Forest of Peace Books, Easton KS 66020.
26. *Sacramentary*, Feast of the Holy Family.
27. *Book of Occasional Services*, Episcopal Church.
28. *Lutheran Book of Worship.*

29. Adapted from *Prayers for the Domestic Church*, copyright © 1979 by Rev. Edward M. Hays, Forest of Peace Books, Easton KS 66020.

30. Copyright © 1981. Office of Liturgy, Diocese of Columbus. All rights reserved.

31. Adapted from a service written by James E. Wilbur, Paluch Pub. Co., Chicago.

32. *Sacramentary*, Solemn Blessing, Passion Sunday.

33. *Sacramentary*, Easter Vigil.

34. *Sacramentary*, Ascension.

35. *Sacramentary*, Pentecost, Vigil Mass.

36. *Book of Family Prayer*, Huck, Seabury Press.

37. *Sacramentary*, Masses and Prayers for Various Needs and Occasions, For the Blessing of Man's Labor.

38. Adapted, *Lutheran Book of Worship*.

39. *Sacramentary*, All Saints.

40. Adapted, *Rite of Baptism for Children*.

41. *Book of Common Prayer*, Episcopal Church.

42. *Sacramentary*, All Souls.

43. *Book of Common Prayer*, Episcopal Church.

44. *Book of Occasional Services*, Episcopal Church.

45. Adapted, *Book of Occasional Services*, Episcopal Church.

46. *Book of Occasional Services*, Episcopal Church.

47. Worship Resources, Inc., 3015 Zuni Street, Denver, CO 80211.

48. *Book of Occasional Services*, Episcopal Church.

49. *Book of Occasional Services*, Episcopal Church.

50. Adapted, *Book of Occasional Services*, Episcopal Church.

51. *Book of Occasional Services*, Episcopal Church.

52. *Book of Occasional Services*, Episcopal Church.

53. Worship Resources, Inc., 3015 Zuni Street, Denver, CO 80211.

54. Worship Resources, Inc., 3015 Zuni Street, Denver, CO 80211.

55. *Book of Occasional Services*, Episcopal Church.

56. *Book of Occasional Services*, Episcopal Church.

57. *Book of Occasional Services*, Episcopal Church.

58. *Book of Occasional Services*, Episcopal Church.

59. *Book of Common Prayer*, Episcopal Church.

60. Translation, German *Book of Blessings*.

61. *Book of Common Prayer*, Episcopal Church.

62. Adapted, *Rite of Baptism for Children*.

63. Adapted, *Rite of Baptism for Children*.

64. Adapted, Worship Resources, Inc., 3015 Zuni Street, Denver, CO 80211.

65. *Sacramentary*, Anniversary of Marriage.

66. *Book of Common Prayer*, Episcopal Church.

67. *Home Celebrations*, Lawrence Moser, SJ, Paulist Press, 1970.

68. Adapted from text by the Liturgical Commission, Diocese of Lansing.

69. *Come, Lord Jesus: Biblical Prayers with Psalms and Scripture Readings* by Lucien Deiss, C.S.Sp., World Library Publications, Chicago, 1981, pp. 298-302.